A TRUE BOOK™

Westward Expansion

TERESA DOMNAUER

Children's Press®
An Imprint of Scholastic Inc.
New York Toronto London Auckland Sydney
Mexico City New Delhi Hong Kong
Danbury, Connecticut

Content Consultant
David R. Smith, Ph.D.
Adjunct Assistant Professor of History
University of Michigan
Ann Arbor, Michigan

Library of Congress Cataloging-in-Publication Data

Domnauer, Teresa.
  Westward expansion / Teresa Domnauer.
    p. cm.—(A true book)
  Includes bibliographical references and index.
  ISBN-13: 978-0-531-20586-0 (lib. bdg.)   978-0-531-21249-3 (pbk.)
  ISBN-10: 0-531-20586-X (lib. bdg.)   0-531-21249-1 (pbk.)

  1. United States—Territorial expansion—Juvenile literature. 2. West
(U.S.)—Discovery and exploration—Juvenile literature. 3. West
(U.S.)—History—19th century—Juvenile literature. 4. Frontier and
pioneer life—West (U.S.)—Juvenile literature. 5. Indians of North
America—West (U.S.)—History—Juvenile literature. 6. Indians of North
America—Government relations—Juvenile literature. 7. Overland
journeys to the Pacific—Juvenile literature. I. Title. II. Series.

E179.5.D654 2010
978'.02—dc22   2009028630

3 4 5 6 7 8 9 10 R 19 18 17 16 15 14 13 12 11   62

Find the Truth!

Everything you are about to read is true *except* for one of the sentences on this page.

Which one is **TRUE**?

T or F The Pony Express was in business for five years.

T or F Between 1841 and 1860, about 300,000 people traveled west on the Oregon Trail.

Find the answers in this book

A Pony Express rider

Contents

A cowboy

The Oregon Trail was about 2,000 miles long and ran from Missouri to Oregon.

THE **BIG** TRUTH!

Remember the Alamo!

5 Pathway to the Pacific

6 The End of the Frontier

A gold miner

5

In 1775, Philadelphia, Pennsylvania, was the largest city in the American colonies.

CHAPTER 1

A Growing Nation

The United States began as a group of 13 **colonies** (KAH-luh-neez) that were ruled by Great Britain. The colonies were located along the East Coast and stretched from New Hampshire in the north to Georgia in the south. They extended as far west as the Appalachian Mountains. Before the late 1700s, few colonists had traveled west of the Appalachians. One hundred years later, the United States would extend west to the Pacific Ocean.

In 1700, there were about 250,000 people living in the colonies. By 1775, there were 2.5 million.

The number of people who settled in the colonies grew quickly.

The Expanding Colonies

People from Europe **migrated** (MY-grate-id) to the colonies, hoping to find better lives. Some came to escape war or poor living conditions in their homelands. Others wanted to be able to own land or to practice their religions freely.

The First Frontier

As the number of people living in the colonies grew, cities and towns became crowded. By the mid-1700s, more living and farming space was needed. So people started spreading west toward the Appalachian Mountains. Native Americans lived in this area, but few other people had explored it. The Appalachians became the 13 colonies' first **frontier** (fruhn-TIHR). As the nation grew, its western **boundary** (BOWN-duh-ree) would be pushed farther and farther out.

This map of the United States in the late 1700s shows the country's western boundary at the Mississippi River.

THE
NORTHWEST TERRITORY, 1787
South Carolina ceded her western
territory to the U. S. in 1787

SCALE OF MILES
0 50 100   200   300   400

Native Americans sometimes defended their land by attacking people moving into the Appalachian Mountains.

A Law for the Land

Great Britain's government thought it would be hard to rule the colonists if they moved farther west. The British also wanted to prevent expensive wars with Native Americans who would defend their land from colonists moving into the Appalachians.

In 1763, Great Britain passed a law called the Proclamation (prah-kluh-MAY-shun) of 1763. The law said that the colonists could not settle beyond the Appalachians. That land would be set aside for Native Americans.

The proclamation angered the colonists. It was one of many reasons why they fought the Revolutionary War against Great Britain, beginning in 1775. In 1776, the colonies announced their **independence** from Great Britain, becoming the United States of America. By 1783, the United States won the war. After the war, all the land west to the Mississippi River, north to Canada, and south to Florida belonged to the United States.

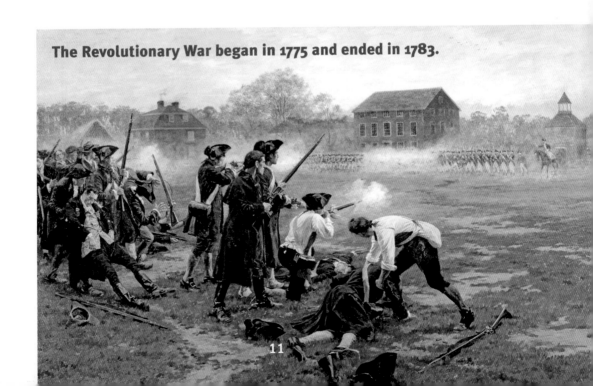

The Revolutionary War began in 1775 and ended in 1783.

Explorer Daniel Boone was also a hunter and caught animals for their furs.

CHAPTER 2

Beyond the Appalachians

Daniel Boone was one **settler** who ignored the Proclamation of 1763. In 1767, Boone left his home in North Carolina to explore what would become the state of Kentucky. By 1775, he helped guide other colonists into this area on a trail that came to be called the Wilderness Road. The trail became the main route for settlers to the Appalachians. In the late 1770s, thousands of people moved west to Kentucky.

Boone and 30 men hacked through the forest with axes to clear the trail that became the Wilderness Road.

The Northwest Territory

After the Revolutionary War, settlers began moving into the Northwest **Territory** (TER-uh-tor-ee). This area included what is today Ohio, Indiana, Illinois, Michigan, Wisconsin, and part of Minnesota. Native American groups that lived there, such as the Shawnee and Miami, fought to defend their land from settlers. In 1794, Native Americans lost the Battle of Fallen Timbers. Their loss caused them to give up their land in present-day Ohio and southeastern Indiana.

Native Americans fight in the Battle of Fallen Timbers.

14

When a territory had 60,000 people living in it, it could apply to become a state.

Government Rules

In 1785, the U.S. government passed a law called the Ordinance (OR-dih-nints) of 1785. This law allowed the government to divide the Northwest Territory into small pieces. The government then sold the land to citizens or businesses.

Two years later, the government passed a set of laws called the Northwest Ordinance. These laws helped set up a government for the Northwest Territory. They outlined rules for how a territory could become a state.

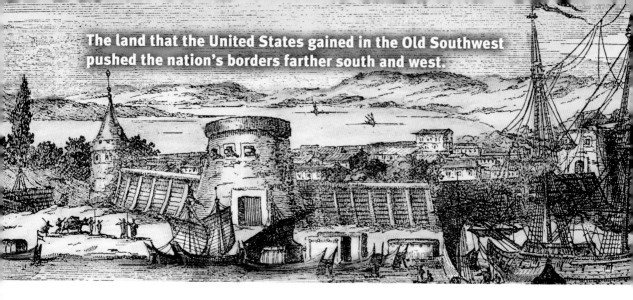
The land that the United States gained in the Old Southwest pushed the nation's borders farther south and west.

The Old Southwest

Another area that the colonists began to settle was called the Old Southwest. At first, the region included present-day Kentucky and Tennessee. It gradually expanded south to the Gulf of Mexico and included today's Louisiana, Mississippi, and Alabama. At this time, Spain controlled what is now the state of Florida. By 1819, Spain had given up its **claim** to Florida and the southern parts of Alabama and Mississippi. The U.S. government also took land from Native Americans in those regions.

The Louisiana Purchase

The U.S. government continued to gain land and expand the country westward. In 1803, the United States paid France $15 million for an enormous section of land called Louisiana. The purchase doubled the size of the United States, and it extended the borders of the country west to the Rocky Mountains and north to Canada. Now there was even more land for Americans to explore and settle.

The land of the Louisiana Purchase became all or parts of 15 U.S. states!

TERRITORY OF LOUISIANA 1803-1819
LOUISIANA PURCHASE TERRITORY ceded by FRANCE to the UNITED STATES by treaty of April 30, 1803, as asserted and maintained by the American Government

During Lewis (left) and Clark's journey through Louisiana Territory, they were helped by Sacagawea (sak-uh-juh-WEE-uh), a Native American woman.

CHAPTER 3

Exploring the West

Explorers, scouts, and hunters helped blaze trails through the new territories of the United States. Two of the most well-known explorers were army captains Meriwether Lewis and William Clark. They were hired by President Thomas Jefferson to explore the land gained in the Louisiana Purchase, beyond the Mississippi River. Lewis and Clark kept journals of their travels. They also created maps of their route that made it possible for others who came after them to find their way west.

Lewis and Clark's trip took more than two years.

Sacagawea

On their journey, Lewis and Clark met a Native American woman named Sacagawea. Sacagawea and her husband joined the **expedition** (ek-spuh-DIH-shun) and helped Lewis and Clark communicate with Native American people. Sacagawea's presence let other Native people know that Lewis and Clark and their men were friendly.

When one of the group's canoes overturned, Sacagawea rescued valuable journals and supplies from the water.

Mountain men were able to find their way through the wilderness without accurate maps.

Davy Crockett was one of the best-known mountain men.

Mountain Men

Fur trappers known as mountain men also ventured into the West in search of valuable beaver fur. As these men hunted for beavers, they discovered new and better routes through the West. Along the way, they faced many dangers, such as starvation and grizzly bear attacks. Sometimes, Native Americans helped them. Mountain men copied Native American clothing, tools, and ways of making food and medicine so they could survive.

James Beckwourth

James (Jim) Beckwourth was an African American mountain man who worked as a fur trapper, guide, and soldier. In 1824, he went on his first fur-trading expedition to the Rocky Mountains. In about 1850, he discovered what would be called Beckwourth Pass. This pathway through the Sierra Nevada mountain range made travel into California much easier. Thousands of settlers used the pass, especially during the California gold rush of the 1840s and 1850s.

USA 29

JIM BECKWOURTH

The U.S. Postal Service issued a postage stamp to honor James Beckwourth in 1994.

22

Words of the West

Jessie Benton Frémont was the wife of explorer John C. Frémont. John **dictated** notes about his western expeditions to Jessie, and she wrote reports that were published in magazines and books. Jessie's reports described the West in a very lively and interesting way. Her writing made the West sound so exciting that many people were inspired to move there.

Thousands of people read Jessie Benton Frémont's writings.

Native Americans fought back against being pushed off their lands.

CHAPTER 4

Native American Struggles

As settlers moved into the new territories, Native Americans continued to be pushed off their lands. President Andrew Jackson wanted the United States to grow. So in 1830, Jackson supported Congress's passage of the Indian Removal Act. This law gave the government the power to force many Native Americans in the East to move as far west as the Mississippi River and beyond.

In 1830, there were 24 U.S. states.

In 1833, Black Hawk's life story became the first Native American autobiography published in the United States.

The Black Hawk War was named for the Sauk leader Black Hawk.

Fight Over Homelands

Despite the Indian Removal Act, many Native American tribes fought hard to stay on their homelands. Between 1817 and 1858, the Seminole Indians of Florida battled the United States in three wars. Eventually, the Seminoles lost. In 1832, the Sauk (SAWK) and Fox tribes fought the Black Hawk War in Illinois and Wisconsin. The Sauk and Fox lost the war to the U.S. Army.

The Trail of Tears

In 1830, the U.S. government began relocating many Native Americans to land known as Indian Territory (present-day Oklahoma). This made it possible for settlers to move onto what had been the Native Americans' land. In 1838, the Cherokee people were forced off their homeland in Georgia. They walked or rode on horseback for 800 mi. (1,287 km) to reach Indian Territory. The route they took became known as the Trail of Tears.

About 16,000 Cherokees were forced to move to Indian Territory on the Trail of Tears.

The Battle of the Little Bighorn

In 1876, U.S. Army officer George Armstrong Custer led an attack on about 2,000 Sioux (SOO) and Cheyenne (SHY-en) warriors in what is now Montana. Custer and his troops were trying to force the tribes to move onto **reservations** (rez-ur-VAY-shunz). The government wanted the tribes' lands. The Battle of the Little Bighorn followed, and Custer and 263 of his men were killed.

The battle got its name because it was fought on the banks of the Little Bighorn River.

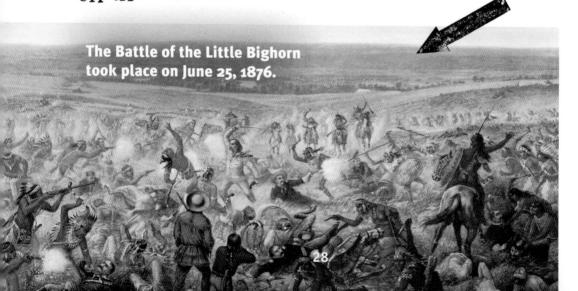

The Battle of the Little Bighorn took place on June 25, 1876.

28

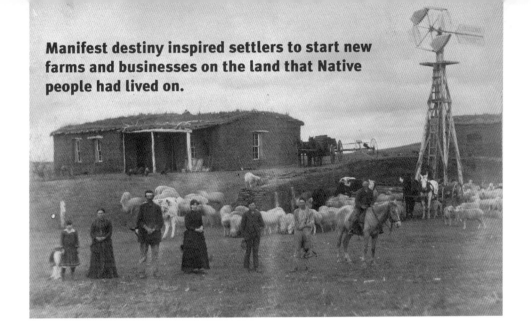
Manifest destiny inspired settlers to start new farms and businesses on the land that Native people had lived on.

The Push for Land

During the 1800s, many Americans thought it was acceptable to push Native Americans off of their land. They believed that Native American lands were needed for all of the people moving west. This idea was called manifest destiny (MAN-uh-fest DESS-tuh-nee). Manifest destiny meant that the U.S. government believed it had the right to expand the country west to the Pacific Ocean—even if Native Americans already lived on the land.

Remember the Alamo!

Battles with Native Americans were not the only conflicts the United States faced as it pushed west. In 1835, Mexico ruled present-day Texas. The Texans didn't want to be ruled by Mexico, so they formed their own country—the Republic of Texas. Mexico and Texas fought a series of battles called the Texas Revolution (1835–1836). During one of the battles, about 200 Texans used a small church in San Antonio as a   . The church became known as the Alamo.

The Battle

For nearly two weeks, 3,000 Mexican soldiers attacked the Alamo. On the final day of the battle, March 6, 1836, nearly all the Texans were killed. Six weeks later, Texas won its independence from Mexico after defeating the Mexicans at the Battle of San Jacinto (HA-seen-toe). The troops' battle cry there was "Remember the Alamo!"

Davy Crockett

In addition to being an explorer, Davy Crockett was a soldier. He died fighting at the Alamo.

In 1848, gold was discovered at Sutter's Mill in Coloma, California. Thousands of people poured into the area hoping to get rich.

CHAPTER 5

Pathway to the Pacific

In the mid-1800s, the United States continued to claim land in the West. Settlers did so for many reasons. The West offered cheap, sometimes free, land. It was a place where religion could be practiced freely. Once gold was discovered in California, it also became a place to get rich. Many businesses and inventions resulted from the growing West and settlers' needs for faster ways to communicate and travel.

 In 1849, $10 million in gold was discovered in California.

Pioneers crossed prairies, deserts, rivers, and mountains as they traveled on the Oregon Trail.

The Oregon Trail

Between 1841 and 1860, about 300,000 people traveled west from Missouri to Oregon Country. They traveled along a route called the Oregon Trail. In a covered wagon, the journey took between four and six months. Some people rode horses, but most walked the entire way. Along the route, travelers faced disease, attacks by Native Americans, harsh weather, and shortages of food and water.

The U.S.-Mexican War

In 1845, the Republic of Texas became a U.S. state. However, Mexico believed it still controlled Texas. Mexico and the United States went to war over Texas the next year. The war ended in 1848, and the two countries signed an agreement. The United States paid Mexico $15 million. Mexico gave up what are now California, Arizona, Nevada, Utah, Texas, and parts of what are now Wyoming, Nebraska, Oklahoma, New Mexico, and Colorado.

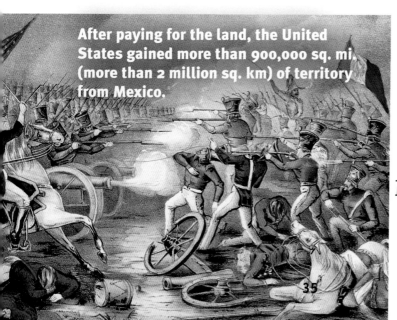

After paying for the land, the United States gained more than 900,000 sq. mi. (more than 2 million sq. km) of territory from Mexico.

The $15 million paid to Mexico would be worth about $313 million today.

35

Freedom of Religion

In 1844, Joseph Smith, the leader of a religious group called the Mormons, was killed by people who did not agree with his religion. Brigham Young became the group's new leader. In 1846, Young led 5,000 Mormons on a long journey west from Missouri to what is now Utah. The Mormons went along, hoping they could practice their religion freely in their new home.

The Mormons founded Salt Lake City, Utah.

Brigham Young led the Mormons to Utah, where they built farms, schools, businesses, and stores.

The Pony Express

From April 1860 to October 1861, the Pony Express delivered mail between Missouri and California. Men on horseback carried the mail 2,000 mi. (3,219 km) in just eight days. Before the Pony Express, it took several weeks for mail to be delivered by stagecoach (a horse-drawn carriage). Once the transcontinental **telegraph** line was completed, messages could be sent very quickly and the Pony Express was no longer needed. Soon, trains also began carrying mail across the country.

A Pony Express rider leaves a general store that serves as a station along a Pony Express route.

Workers from the United States, Ireland, and China helped build the transcontinental railroad.

60

CHAPTER 6

The End of the Frontier

By the late 1800s, the United States stretched from the East Coast to the West Coast. No more frontier remained to be settled. As people were learning to live together in new surroundings, new rules and laws were made to help them. Also during this time, new developments, such as the transcontinental railroad, allowed for travel to become easier and faster and for businesses to grow.

 The total length of the railroad was 1,776 mi. (2,858 km).

The Wild West

The West was a rough place where people had to be strong to work and survive. Rugged cowboys spent long days on horseback herding cattle or sheep. They faced dangers such as cattle **stampedes** and being thrown from wild horses called broncos. Gunfighters were the police officers of the West. With guns at their sides, they protected the townspeople from criminals called outlaws.

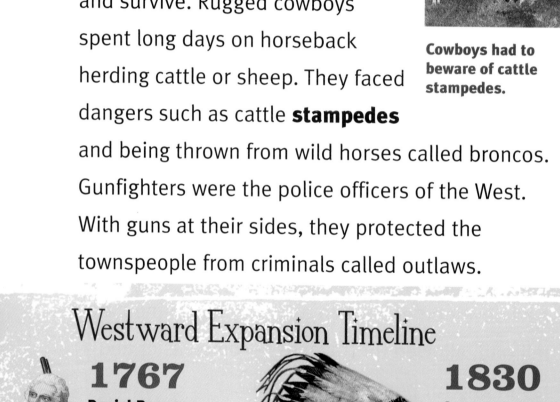

Cowboys had to beware of cattle stampedes.

Westward Expansion Timeline

1767
Daniel Boone explores Kentucky for the first time.

1830
Congress passes the Indian Removal Act.

Buffalo Bill

The wild and tough West became the subject of shows staged by William Frederick Cody. Also known

A poster from Buffalo Bill's Wild West Show

as Buffalo Bill, Cody had served in the U.S. Army and had been a bison hunter. His Buffalo Bill's Wild West Show featured horse races, rodeo-style events, and performances of battles with Native Americans.

1846–1848
The United States fights the U.S.–Mexican War.

1890
The U.S. government announces that all the land in the West has been explored.

A New Nation

Before the late 1700s, most Americans did not know what the West was like. One hundred years later, in 1890, the U.S. government stated that there was no more frontier left to settle in the West. From coast to coast, the United States had filled up with towns, cities, farms, and ranches built by people as they moved west. What was once the 13 colonies had grown into one of the largest nations in the world. ★

Denver, Colorado, grew into a busy city as people moved west.

42

True Statistics

Name of Daniel Boone's settlement in Kentucky: Boonesborough

Cost to send a letter by Pony Express: $5.00 at first, then the price dropped to $1.00

Original name of Texas: The Lone Star Republic

Year that California became a state: 1850

Another name for the Battle of the Little Bighorn: Custer's Last Stand

Size of the Louisiana Purchase: 828,800 sq. mi. (more than 2 million sq. km)

Location of the Alamo: San Antonio, Texas

Did you find the truth?

(F) The Pony Express was in business for five years.

(T) Between 1841 and 1860, about 300,000 people traveled west on the Oregon Trail.

Resources

Books

Feeney, Kathy. *Davy Crockett*. Mankato, MN: Bridgestone Books, 2002.

January, Brendan. *The Thirteen Colonies*. New York: Children's Press, 2000.

Kalman, Bobbie. *Life on the Trail*. New York: Crabtree Publishing Company, 1999.

Markel, Rita J. *Your Travel Guide to America's Old West*. Minneapolis: Lerner Publications Company, 2004.

Miller, Jay. *American Indian Families*. New York: Children's Press, 1996.

Nobleman, Marc Tyler. *The Battle of Little Bighorn*. Minneapolis: Compass Point Books, 2002.

Nobleman, Marc Tyler. *The Mexican War*. Minneapolis: Compass Point Books, 2005.

Salas, Laura Purdie. *The Wilderness Road, 1775*. Mankato, MN: Bridgestone Books, 2003.

Suen, Anastasia. *Trappers & Mountain Men*. Vero Beach, FL: Rourke Publishing, 2007.

Webster, Christine. *The Lewis and Clark Expedition* (Cornerstones of Freedom, Second Series). New York: Children's Press, 2003.

Organizations and Web Sites

The Alamo: Just for Kids
www.thealamo.org/just_for_kids.html
Find puzzles, games, and information about the Alamo at this site.

Buffalo Bill Museum
www.bbhc.org/bbm/
Learn about Buffalo Bill Cody and read more about the West.

Historic Oregon City: End of the Oregon Trail
www.historicoregoncity.org/HOC/
Find answers to questions about the Oregon Trail and the pioneers.

Places to Visit

Museum of the Mountain Man
770 E. Hennick
Pinedale, WY 82941
(877) 686-6266
www.museumofthemountainman.com

View items from mountain men and Native Americans.

National Museum of the American Indian
Fourth Street & Independence Ave., S.W.
Washington, DC 20560
(202) 633-1000
www.nmai.si.edu

Explore Native American art in the galleries and sample Native American food at the café.

Important Words

boundary (BOWN-duh-ree) – something that marks the edge or limit

claim – a right to own something

colonies (KAH-luh-neez) – places where groups of people come to settle that are under the control of their home country

dictated – said or read aloud for someone to write down

expedition (ek-spuh-DIH-shun) – a journey taken for a reason

fort – a strong building used during battles for protection and defense

frontier (fruhn-TIHR) – the far edge of a country, where few people live

independence – freedom from being controlled by someone else

migrated (MY-grate-id) – moved from one region into another

reservations (rez-ur-VAY-shunz) – areas of land set aside by the U.S. government for Native Americans to live on

settler – a person who makes a home in a new area

stampedes – the sudden and fast movements of a large group of animals

telegraph – a device or system for sending messages over long distances. It uses a code of electrical signals sent by wire.

territory (TER-uh-tor-ee) – an area of land that belongs to and is governed by a country

Index

Page numbers in **bold** indicate illustrations

About the Author

Teresa Domnauer is the author of many nonfiction books for children. She has a bachelor's degree in creative writing from Emerson College and received her teaching certification from Ohio Dominican University. Ms. Domnauer lives in Connecticut with her husband, Brendon, and their two daughters, Ellie and Robin.